I0622780

MINDSET OF THE MASTERS

HOW TO DEVELOP THE MINDSET OF SUCCESS

MIRIAM JONES

REALLY**EDUCATED**

REALLY**EDUCATED**

This book is not intended to provide personalized legal, accounting, financial, mental or emotional health, therapy, or investment advice. Readers are encouraged to seek the counsel of competent professionals regarding such matters as interpretation of the law, proper accounting procedures, financial planning, mental health counseling, personal therapy, and investment strategies. The Author and Publisher specifically disclaim any liability, loss, or risk which is incurred as a consequence, directly or indirectly, of the use and application of any of the contents of this work.

MINDSET OF THE MASTERS. Copyright © 2023 by Miriam Jones. All rights reserved. Printed in the United States of America. No part of this book may be used or reproduced in any manner whatsoever without written permission except in the case of brief quotations embodied in critical articles and reviews.

ISBN: 979-8-9880973-8-9 (e-book)

979-8-9880973-9-6 (paperback)

www.reallyeducated.com

This is for the ones who seek clarity. The ones who are on their path to greatness and ready to embrace all that life has for them.

CONTENTS

DEVELOPING THE MINDSET OF SUCCESS

Have you ever wondered what makes some people successful while others try their best but never really get there? Have you been challenging yourself to do better and achieve your goals?

If so, then *Mindset of the Masters: How to Develop the Mindset of Success* is for you. This book will help guide you from where you are to where you want to be.

If you are ready to take your life from ordinary to extraordinary, follow along and learn how to think like a winner.

1

FINDING YOUR WHY

The journey to success begins with purpose.

— MIRIAM JONES

The journey to success begins with purpose. What is your reason for being? The answer to that question creates the framework for your vision, which can be filled in by taking action.

Discovering your why can be exciting, but how exactly is it done? The process involves reflection and an honest evaluation of the core values and abilities that you bring to the table. To uncover your purpose, you must release any negative thinking and open your heart and mind to acceptance of yourself.

What is it that drives you? What are your natural abilities, and how can they be used to positively impact the world around you? Taking inventory of the skills you possess and the desires that drive you will unlock the door to discovering ways to use these gifts to help others.

Once you become aware of who you are and your reason for living, you are ready to begin building on that knowledge through consistent personal development and mindset strengthening.

Ways to Discover Your Purpose

- Meditation and quiet reflection
- Seeking revelation from a higher source
- Understanding your strengths and weaknesses
- Embracing your natural abilities

Declarations

1. I am who I am meant to be.
2. I have all that I need to be successful.
3. I know who I am and why I am here.

Action Steps

1. Spend 10 minutes each morning in quiet reflection and embrace the essence of your existence.
2. Take a personality assessment this week to discover your core values and skills.
3. Make a list of your strengths. Be intentional about incorporating them into your daily routine.

2

CRAFTING A PLAN

After you have discovered your purpose, the next step is to craft a plan. What are your goals? Take a few moments to brainstorm ideas. Once you are finished, rank your goals from largest to smallest and assign each a timeframe for completion.

Think about how achieving these objectives makes you feel. Fully experiencing this excitement will help you connect emotionally with your vision. Having an emotional attachment to your cause is important, as that is what will keep you motivated when things don't seem to line up.

When you have a plan in place, whatever is necessary to complete it will flow to you as you take one step at a time. Your dedication to doing what it takes to accomplish what you have in mind will give you the confidence needed to take risks. You will begin to value completing your mission over any discomfort or fear that might try to creep in.

Having an emotional attachment to your cause is important, as that is what will keep you motivated when things don't seem to line up.

Craft Your Plan

1. Make a list of things that you would like to accomplish.
2. Narrow it down to three items.
3. Pick out the top goal that you would like to achieve and assign it a completion date.
4. Each day, take action to move forward.

Declarations

1. My goals are attainable.
2. My desires work together with my purpose.
3. I can do whatever is necessary to make my plan a reality.

Action Steps

1. After you have written out your top goal, come up with three specific actions that you can take to get started.
2. Share your plan with a friend, mentor, or accountability partner.
3. Each morning, look in the mirror and declare how reaching your goal makes you feel.

3

ILLUMINATE YOUR MIND

Mindset is everything. What you think determines how you act. The actions you take determine the results you get. So, to achieve the goals that you have set for yourself, you must believe that they are possible.

Thinking and believing are two different things. You can think about accomplishing great things, but unless you know that it is possible for you, it is unlikely to happen. The way that you turn thinking into belief is by living as if you already have what you are trying to get.

Your mind is rational by default. It takes in the current environment, and the body responds accordingly. What you must do is retrain your brain to align not with how things are today, but with what you want them to be in the future.

Consistently inputting positive and progressive thoughts into your mind will allow you to function at a higher level. Once you make the decision to elevate your thinking, things will begin to fall into place. You will feel more confident and less distracted by your current situation because your focus has shifted from the present to the possible.

To achieve the goals that you have set for yourself, you must believe that they are possible.

How to Elevate Your Thinking

- Recite affirmative declarations.
- Surround yourself with positive people.
- Visualize the completion of your goals.
- Consume inspirational literature and music.

Declarations

1. I am grateful for all that I have and all that I am.
2. I am so blessed to have
   _____. (Fill in the blank with what you desire.)
3. I believe in my dream.

Action Steps

1. This week, download a daily positivity app. Take time in the morning to reflect on the quotes.
2. Practice visualizing what fulfilling your purpose looks like.

3. Join an online group of like-minded individuals that supports your vision of success.

4
_____

SPREAD YOUR WINGS

You've shifted your mindset. Now it is time to put your confidence, skills, and plan into action. This is the step that holds many people back for various reasons. The easiest way to get started is to find one thing that you can do each day that will bring you closer to accomplishing your goals. Here are a few ideas to get you going.

Learn

Never stop learning, and always prioritize personal development. As you grow and change, you increase your capacity to reach higher levels of success. Reading is critical to expanding your mind and sharpening your focus.

Engage

The connections you make will determine the breadth of your impact. Although we are all equipped with a unique gift, we are also limited by our personal abilities. Having a strong network of people around you that specialize in things that you do not, makes life easier, more efficient, and more productive.

Write

Keeping track of your progress and feelings is a great way to maintain balance and understand what is working and what is not. Each day, take time to write out what you achieved, what you failed at, and how it made you feel. Healthy expression stimulates creativity and frees your mind and body of unnecessary stress.

As you implement these steps into your daily routine, you will notice a difference in the way you act, feel, and think. These changes are necessary for your elevation to new levels of accomplishment.

Find one thing that you can do each day that will bring you closer to accomplishing your goals.

Take Action

- Gain knowledge and become an expert.
- Increase your influence by making connections.
- Spend time attending events and volunteering.
- Keep a journal tracking your progress and adjust daily.

Declarations

1. I am an action taker.
2. I am so happy to be connected to the right people.
3. My gifts are meaningful and impactful.

Action Steps

1. Schedule time to attend an event or webinar this week that will increase your knowledge on a topic of interest.
2. Purchase a journal and begin keeping entries every evening, recapping the day.
3. Reconnect with one person in your network that you have not engaged with in the past three months.

5

THERE ARE NO MISTAKES

One of the biggest hurdles that keeps people from trying new things or making progress is the fear of failure. Even the most intelligent individuals can get stuck overthinking. A lesson that I learned while working with successful people is that you cannot mess up.

A mentor of mine used the example of an electrician. He or she had to start somewhere. They did not come out the gate knowing everything. It may have even started with learning how to screw in a lightbulb. As simple as it may seem, it is true. Everyone starts somewhere.

There is no need to compare yourself to others' progress. It is all a process. The speed at which you advance is dependent on your ability to adapt. Learning takes place through both failure and success. The more that you practice using your talents and pursuing things that match up with your purpose, the easier it becomes to overcome fear and overthinking.

Everyone starts somewhere.

Things to Remember

- Life is not a competition.
- You have everything you need to fulfill your purpose.
- Often, no one will notice your errors because they are either too focused on their own lives to be concerned or they are relieved that you took the initiative, so they don't have to.

Declarations

1. There are no mistakes.
2. Life is about learning.
3. I accept the challenge to grow.

Action Steps

1. This week, research 3–5 successful people. Write down the commonalities that they share.
2. Make a list of the top three things that challenge you and decide what actions you will take to overcome them.
3. Pick one thing that you have never done before and do it.

6

WATCH YOUR ENERGY

Your surroundings matter. A big influence on success is who you are connected to. Make it a point to nurture the positive relationships in your life and put yourself in a position to receive opportunities for collaboration.

You do not have to know it all, and really, it can be beneficial if you don't. Having access to the best talent in various capacities will multiply your effectiveness and ability to elevate.

Over time, we become who we hang around. There is no room for negative energy or small thinking on the road to greatness. Guard your mind and heart because your future success depends on them.

There is no room for negative energy or small thinking on the road to greatness.

Find People Who

- Support your dream
- Have a compatible mindset
- Are consistent and reliable communicators
- Are pursuing their own dreams
- Function from a place of integrity

Declarations

1. I choose to surround myself with positivity.
2. I release anything that is not for me.
3. I have strong connections.

Action Steps

1. Make a list of three ways that you can reach out to your network this month.
2. Categorize your connections in the following order: core connections, inner circle, acquaintances, business associates, and allies.
3. Handwrite personal notes for each of your core connections and mail them off this week.

7

ASK FOR WHAT YOU WANT

J ust like there are no mistakes in trying, there are no limits to your ability to ask for what you desire. Many times, people are ashamed to truly articulate their expectations and end up settling for less than they require. Whether it is in business, relationships, or life in general, being able to determine your needs prior to engaging and not shortchanging yourself is crucial.

One thing that I have learned is that you cannot lose if you stick to your standards. But to do so, you must know what those are. When you determine what a fair ask is, the fear of rejection decreases. This is because you lose nothing by asking and gain everything if your request is granted.

From this day forward, make the decision that you will be deliberate in going for exactly what you want or need, and understand that not every opportunity will be able to deliver that.

You cannot lose if you stick to your standards.

Keys to Getting What You Desire

- Develop communication and negotiation skills.
- Understand that not every deal will be right for you.
- Know your standards ahead of time.
- Never settle for less.

Declarations

1. I know my worth.
2. I know what I want.
3. I value my time and honor my feelings.

Action Steps

1. Before you enter your next transaction, take time to review your requirements and make it a point to adhere to them.
2. Reflect on the areas of your life where you have compromised. Write down three ways that you can do better.
3. Think about the thing that you desire most. What are you willing to do to get it?

8

BRING YOUR OWN SEAT

There will be times when you need to take initiative. While I do not suggest forcing things to happen, sometimes you need to position yourself to receive all that is available to you. It can be easy to make excuses out of fear or a lack of confidence, however, if you are to elevate, you must learn to adapt.

I have encountered many uncomfortable situations, and each experience taught me how to think on my toes, be resourceful, and communicate. When you get around people who function at a higher level, you begin to see just how differently things work in certain realms.

However, perhaps one of the most encouraging observations is that, at the end of the day, we are all still humans. No matter the title, accomplishments, accolades, or prestige, we all face challenges. The difference is that most never get to see behind the curtain. For this reason, do not be afraid to step into the room, even if you must bring your own seat.

At the end of the day, we are all still humans.

Ways to Position Yourself

- Attend in-person meetups or virtual events.
- Schedule free consultations with coaches or industry leaders.
- Reach out via email and introduce yourself.

Declarations

1. I know what I bring to the table.
2. I am worthy of being in the room.
3. I am grateful for the opportunities that come my way.

Action Steps

1. Write down three unique things about yourself and why they are important.
2. Sign up for and attend a local or virtual personal development event.
3. Pick one person to introduce yourself to this week.

IT'S NOT A COMPETITION

G et comfortable embracing each day as it comes, always understanding the bigger picture. As you walk your path, it is very important not to become overly concerned with your progress as compared to those around you.

Comparison causes distraction. Learn, collaborate, encourage, and inspire, but do not fall victim to jealousy, division, competition, or sabotage.

Your path is the right path for you. Along the way, others will contribute to and help you, but at the end of the day, what makes you special is your ability to carry out your purpose without compromise.

Comparison causes distraction.

How to Stay Focused

- Understand your value.
- Set new goals as you complete old ones.

- Become your biggest fan.

Declarations

1. I fully embrace my purpose.
2. My life path is unique.
3. I am focused on my journey.

Action Steps

1. Each morning, write down three things that you are grateful for.
2. Are there areas in your life where you compare yourself to others? If so, what are some ways that you can resolve this?
3. Think of someone you know who needs help. Reach out them this week and offer assistance.

WALK BY FAITH

You've discovered the importance of reshaping your thoughts and training your mind with positivity. But inevitably, unexpected circumstances will arise. During those moments, it is important not to get stuck focusing on the situation.

Instead, remember that what you cannot control should not control you. Release the pressure and stress associated with the unpredictable and embrace the knowledge that there is a higher reason for your season.

Likewise, if you are to soar to new heights, it is important that you be able to understand where your human limitations intersect with the supernatural. The belief that your goals are achievable may go beyond what you see physically, but unless you are able to have faith that they will come to pass, they very well may not.

Don't miss out on fulfilling your potential because you failed to open yourself to the possibilities.

What you cannot control should not control you.

How to Have Faith

- Understand that there are things that you cannot control.
- Be okay with releasing responsibility for the unforeseeable.
- Know that every occurrence is meaningful.
- Trust that what is meant to happen will.

Declarations

1. I release control over the things I cannot change.
2. I believe that I can achieve my goals.
3. I am committed to walking by faith.

Action Steps

1. Each morning, take time for quiet reflection and release any stress or anxiety you may have.
2. Write down three things that you believe in.
3. Reflect on what your beliefs are and how they can help guide you.

7 KEYS

Congratulations on developing your mindset for success! Along the way, you have gained valuable insight and uncovered helpful tips to guide your path.

Here are 7 final reminders to keep you motivated:

- Mindset is the key that unlocks the door of possibility.
- Obstacles are opportunities to expand your potential.
- You become the company you keep.
- You can't eat if you don't open your mouth.
- No one is better, just different.
- The path you walk is unique. Don't be distracted.
- Trust the process even when you don't see progress.

Remember, the seed that you sow today will

continue to grow with the right nurture and time. Stay committed to your goal.

SHARE THE SUCCESS

"Be the light that helps others find their way."

— MIRIAM JONES

Success is not a solo sport. Even though it begins with the development of your inner thoughts and desires, elevation requires engagement.

If you know someone who would be enlightened by this content, please share it with them. As you put positive energy into the atmosphere, it opens the space for positivity to flow back to you.

I wish you continued peace and success on your journey.

Live Life. Be Happy. Dream Big.

ABOUT THE AUTHOR

Miriam Jones is an American author who creates content that helps people learn how to live a life of fulfillment and purpose. Although she holds degrees in marketing and law, Miriam's greatest passion is using her gifts to inspire others to succeed. Her works focus on presenting information in a way that is simple, practical, and encouraging. Readers are challenged to put what they have learned into immediate action which creates accelerated results.

ALSO BY MIRIAM JONES

www.ingramcontent.com/pod-product-compliance
Lightning Source LLC
Chambersburg PA
CBHW020347130626
46549CB00003B/1336